THE IRISH
COUNTRY HOUSE

By The Knight of Glin and James Peill

Photographs by James Fennell

Thames & Hudson

CONTENTS

Introduction

THE HOUSES AND CASTLES THAT FORM THE SUBJECT OF THIS BOOK ARE
all still owned and lived in by the descendants of the people who built them. This in
itself is a major achievement, given Ireland's turbulent history and the rise and fall
of its precarious economy. The roll call of Irish country houses still in their original
family's ownership has diminished to such an extent that desperate cries have gone out
to save them before there are none left. Even since Hugh Montgomery-Massingberd
and Christopher Simon Sykes's beautiful book *Great Houses of Ireland* came out
ten years ago, one of the houses featured (Lissadell) has been sold by its owners, the
Gore-Booths. More recently, Carrigglas, featured in Jacqueline O'Brien and Desmond
Guinness's *Great Irish Houses and Castles* (1992), has passed out of the Lefroys' hands
and now remains gaunt and empty, its gardens overgrown and an unsuccessful golf
and housing project left unfinished. In the three decades since Desmond Guinness's
earlier book *Irish Houses and Castles* (1971), written with William Ryan, three of the
houses featured have been sold (Malahide Castle, Newbridge House, and Abbey Leix)
and one destroyed by fire (Powerscourt). Many others can be added to the list, perhaps
the most significant sale being that of Adare Manor, the seat of the Earls of Dunraven,
featured in the German book *Irish Houses* published in 1982 (and in English in 1984).
But the sales of Irish landed estates are not a recent phenomenon; in fact their origins
can be traced back to the beginning of the nineteenth century as we discussed in our
book *Irish Furniture* (2007).

The fortunes of the Irish aristocracy went into decline after the Act of Union
in 1800 (whereby the kingdoms of Great Britain and Ireland were united) and were
further reduced during the Great Famine (c. 1845–50). Prince Hermann von Pückler-
Muskau visited Ireland in 1828 and revealed that many country houses were already
on a downward turn. He gave an apt description of the ramshackle Bermingham in
Co. Galway, "the rain (for alas it does rain) runs merrily through my windows, and falls
in romantic cascades from the windowsill to the floor, where the old carpet thirstily
drinks the stream. The furniture is rather tottery."

After a brief period of recovery in the 1860s and early 1870s, the onset of economic
depression, accompanied by the growth of various land movements from the late

1870s, marked the beginning of the end for the Irish country house. Under the 1881 Land Act, tenants were granted fixity of tenure and fair rents, which inevitably meant lower rents. Under the terms of this and later land acts, particularly the 1903 Wyndham Land Act, a revolutionary transfer of land ownership took place in Ireland. When the post–World War I economic depression wiped out the capital received from these land sales, the country house, which had previously been financed from the rent of many thousands of acres, was now obliged to survive on the income derived from a few hundred acres within the original demesne walls. Novelist George Moore, a landowner in Co. Mayo, put the situation bleakly in 1887, pointing out that all the income of these landlords came from the unending, grinding labor of the miserable peasants. He painted the picture:

In Ireland, the passage, direct and brutal, from the horny hands of the peasant, to the delicate hands of the proprietor, is terribly suggestive of serfdom. In England the landlord lays out the farm and builds the farm buildings; in Ireland, he does absolutely nothing. He gives the bare land to the peasant and sends his agent in to collect the half-yearly rent; in a word, he allows the peasant to keep him in ease and luxury. . . . In Ireland, every chicken eaten, every glass of champagne drunk, every silk dress trailed in the street, every rose worn at a ball, comes straight out of the peasant's cabin.

The Settled Land Act of 1882 freed the hitherto restrictive entailments and allowed owners to dispose of their heirlooms, resulting in an avalanche of sales denuding ancestral homes of works of art, furniture, and libraries. The War of Independence and Civil War of 1920–23 saw the burning of many country houses. After these so-called Troubles, Ireland became an economic backwater and slowly the power of the Anglo-Irish (as the owners of these houses were known) waned away and the demesnes were divided up by the Land Commission. Elderly people tried to make ends meet in their great houses, often moving from room to room as the roof leaked and then gave in. The public tide was heavily against them, as the words of Seán Moylan (a member of the Irish National Parliament) spoken to the Dáil in 1941 made clear: "But, in general, the majority of these big houses that I know, and I am very familiar with them, are not structurally sound, have no artistic value and no historic interest. From my unregenerate point of view, I choose to regard them as tombstones of a departed ascendancy and the sooner they go down the better. They are no use." Heavy inheritance taxation by the Irish government in the 1970s sounded the death knell for many country houses, crippled already by lack of funds. When Charlie Clements inherited Killadoon from his father's cousin, a staggering 55 percent tax on the value of the estate was due, followed by a further 40 percent on the remainder once his cousin Kitty, who had a life interest in the estate, had died.

The houses in this book demonstrate the distinct architectural character of the Irish country house. Many of the early houses incorporated former castles and tower houses, as is the case at Birr and Huntington. Toward the end of the seventeenth century the need for defense diminished, and classical architecture began to flourish, particularly under the patronage of the great James Butler, Duke of Ormonde, Lord Lieutenant of Ireland. His seat was Kilkenny Castle, and detailed inventories show that the rooms were hung with tapestries, chandeliers, notable portraits, elaborate gilt furnishings, silver sconces, and much more. During this period, the formal gardens at Killruddery were created in the French style of André Le Nôtre, reminiscent of the gardens at Courances, near Paris. Pakenham Hall, now known as Tullynally, had a formal canal with stepped cascades and basins in front of the fairly modest house that forms the core of the Gothic revival castle seen today.

The Irish architect Sir Edward Lovett Pearce, whose mother was a cousin of the English architect Sir John Vanbrugh, brought the Palladian style to Ireland and was involved with the extraordinarily grand Castletown, Co. Kildare—not far from Killadoon, a typical plain and well-proportioned country house of the 1760s. Glin was similarly a plain, many-windowed Georgian house with notable neoclassical interiors, later transformed into a gimcrack Gothic castle in the 1820s by the addition of crenellation and little else. Known as baronial architecture, this sort of Gothicizing of houses became popular in the nineteenth century. Glin's exterior plainness belies what lies inside; this is another characteristic of Irish country houses: plain on the outside, except for the front door. Tarbert House, not far from Glin, is also a fairly simple mid-eighteenth-century box on the outside, but retains some important paneled interiors. These fairly modest houses still survive all over Ireland and are livable and cozy places. Burtown, the family home of our photographer, James Fennell, is just such a house, with an eccentric and somewhat illogical arrangement of rooms and fenestration. The interior has delightfully provincial neoclassical plasterwork, laurel-wreathed medallions, and four oddly placed busts in each corner of the hall.

Ireland produced some notable early-nineteenth-century architects, such as Francis Johnston, Sir Richard Morrison, and his son William Vitruvius Morrison, all of whom were equally at home in the Gothic and classical idioms. Two of these, Francis Johnston and Richard Morrison, worked at Tullynally, together with James Sheil, a lesser known exponent of the Gothic style. At Birr the 2nd Earl of Rosse was his own architect, assisted by the almost unrecorded John Johnston. Brothers James and George Robert Pain, pupils of John Nash, had an extensive practice in the

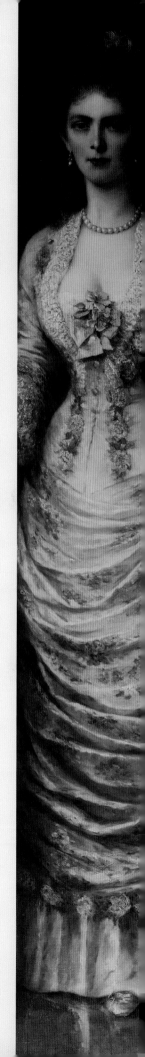

southwest, and James was probably responsible for the cloak of baronial detailing at Glin.

How did the ancestors of the owners of these houses end up in Ireland? The Knights of Glin, originally a Norman family, have been at Glin since the thirteenth century and have always considered themselves more rooted to the Irish soil than the later waves of settlers. These include the Elizabethan Planters, colonists such as the Brabazons who arrived in the mid-sixteenth century, and the Parsons, who came at the end of the century. Members of each family held government office. John Esmonde was Bishop of Ferns, Co. Wexford, in the mid-fourteenth century. The first of the Fennells in Ireland was a soldier, as was the first Pakenham. The Clements were soldiers in Oliver Cromwell's army. Many Scottish families settled in Ireland—particularly in Ulster in the seventeenth century—such as the Leslies of Tarbert, the McClintocks, and the Blackwoods. Most of the ascendancy, as the landed class was known, were of English or Scottish extraction, with very few of native Gaelic origin. Today, the O'Conors, the O'Briens, and the O'Gradys are among those who still retain ownership of small parts of their original lands. Indeed, hardly any members of the ascendancy now have enough land to support their family homes. The small selection of families in this sample owned nearly 200,000 acres in 1878. This has dwindled to a few thousand at most. As far back as 1874, the 1st Marquess of Dufferin and Ava proclaimed: "An Irish estate is like a sponge and an Irish landlord is never so rich as when he is rid of his property." In his seminal book, *The Decline of the Big House in Ireland, a Study of Irish Landed Families 1860–1960* (2001), historian Terence Dooley gives a vivid historical account of the demise of the landlord class. Today in the south of Ireland there are only two large estates: Curraghmore and Lismore. Most others are the original demesne land, often as little as 400 or 500 acres; unless their owners marry money or are entrepreneurial, there is little to support the Irish country house.

There has been recent change under the Celtic Tiger, the nickname for the buoyant Irish economy of recent times. Some houses like Stackallan, Charleville, Lyons, Castletown Cox, Ardbraccan, and Abbey Leix have been bought by cultivated businessmen and have seen a renaissance of their fortunes. They now house important collections of Irish furniture and paintings. The new owners of Lissadel, with far-sighted enthusiasm, bought many of the original contents and have completed the restoration of the house and gardens. The founding of the Irish Heritage Trust should have been a clarion call for the preservation of houses and estates whose owners could not afford to keep them going. Fota was their first success and received support from the government and a private foundation. However, even this brief respite in the fortunes of the houses has taken a dramatic downturn. The gardens at Annesgrove were in line to be taken over by the Trust, until the end of 2008 when the true state of Ireland's finances became horribly apparent.

The late John Cornforth, in a perspicacious 1976 article in *Country Life*, "Tourism and Irish Houses," wrote:

With planning and preservation arrangements in town and country still in their infancy, there is nothing to stop a purchaser buying a historic demesne for its land, splitting it up, developing it and abandoning the house. Also, there is no effective machinery to prevent the export of works of art, including Irish pictures and furniture. In view of all this and despite all that might be felt about what the country house represented in the past, historic houses and demesnes in Ireland are of themselves vital agents for preservation and they must be seen as such; the results of collapse would be catastrophic.

Since this was written, planning acts have passed but are sadly not always adhered to. During the Celtic Tiger, many Irish works of art were repatriated, but this changed after the economic downturn. In the case of Glin, the collection of Irish pictures and works of art not original to the house have been sold in order to keep the property going. Bantry is a similar case. The tourist value of many of these houses is of great importance to Ireland's economy. The Irish Georgian Society has recently been active with Fáilte Ireland, the National Tourism Development Authority, in setting up a forum for the various bodies involved with built heritage. In addition, the Irish Historic Houses Association has been formed for all the houses in Ireland still owned by the original families. They usefully concern themselves with taxation matters, hold important meetings, and publish a regular newsletter.

The future for the ten houses in this book will be difficult. The owners will have to use great energy and enterprise to keep them going; many have already begun to take guests and host events in an effort to sustain the properties. But at the moment, these houses are well loved by the descendants of their original owners. The atmospheric photographs in this book bring to life the layered history of each house and illuminate the fascinating and often eccentric lives of the people who once occupied them.

PAGE 1: *Detail of a bellpull at Killadoon.*

PAGES 2–3: *A view of Killruddery from across the parklike gardens.*

PAGES 4–5: *The sculpture gallery at Killruddery designed in 1852 by William Burn to house the marbles collected by the 10th Earl of Meath on his Grand Tour.*

PAGE 6: *Detail of a portrait of Queen Henrietta Maria, reflected in a mirror at Birr Castle.*

PAGE 7: *Detail of a portrait at Glin Castle of Colonel John FitzGerald, 23rd Knight of Glin, by Joseph Wilson, 1782.*

PAGE 8: *Detail of a portrait at Glin Castle of Sir John King, 1st Baron Kingston, attributed to John Michael Wright.*

PAGE 9: *Detail of a portrait in the dining room at Clandeboye of Hariot, wife of Frederick, 1st Marquess of Dufferin and Ava.*

OPPOSITE: *Detail of a portrait at Killadoon of Hannah Gore, wife of Nathaniel Clements, by Charles Jervas.*

RIGHT: *Detail of a portrait at Killruddery of Anthony Brabazon, 14th Earl of Meath in his Grenadier Guards' uniform.*

Birr Castle

COUNTY OFFALY

Suddenly, at about three in the morning, there was a little tap at the door, and there were two little people with their suitcases, saying the house was on fire. Oh dear, oh dear, what had happened? In fact, the central heating had got so hot that the wallpaper had peeled off and fallen over the four-poster bed. Poor things, they thought it was the house on fire. It was just one of those things that happens in an Irish house.

Presiding over the Georgian town of Birr is the Gothic silhouette of the castle, seat of the Parsons family, Earls of Rosse, since 1620. But this forbidding exterior is misleading, for to enter through the Gothic iron gates in the encircling demesne wall is to enter an enchanted world where there is everything to delight the eye. It has not always been so peaceful. The castle was besieged in 1641 for fifteen months during the Irish Rebellion and again in 1689 during the Williamite War. Fortunately, the seventeenth-century yew-wood staircase survived, noted in 1681 as "the fairest staircase in Ireland" by the English topographer Thomas Dineley.

The castle was originally the stronghold of the O'Carroll family, lords of the area known as Ely O'Carroll; their medieval tower house was later incorporated into a larger mansion by Sir Laurence Parsons. As a charming drawing in Lady Parsons's cookbook of 1668 depicts, the castle faced onto the town with a bawn and flankers at the rear

and a terrace leading up to the front door. A plasterwork frieze with masks and foliage swags survives from this date in the present-day muniments room; this houses one of the most important collections of family papers remaining in private hands in Ireland.

It was during the more tranquil times of the eighteenth century that the orientation of the castle was changed to face out across a landscaped park created by Sir Laurence Parsons, 3rd Baronet. Sir Laurence was the

ABOVE: *The huge heraldic entrance gates were designed by Mary, Countess of Rosse, a pioneering photographer.*

PRECEDING PAGES: *The crenellated profile of Birr Castle overlooking the River Camcor, which is spanned by Ireland's first suspension bridge.*

OPPOSITE: *A Gothic bedroom corridor lined with family portraits.*

RIGHT: *The muniments room still has the original seventeenth-century plasterwork frieze.*

OPPOSITE: *Many fascinating documents are housed in the muniments room, including Lady Parsons's cookbook of 1668 depicting the castle, then called Parsonstown House.*

BELOW: *Lady Bridget Parsons, daughter of the 5th Earl of Rosse.*

BOTTOM: *The Birr bourgeoisie painted by the young Lady Alicia Parsons, daughter of the 2nd Earl of Rosse, in the 1820s.*

OVERLEAF: *The great Gothic music room.*

patron of his young cousin Samuel Chearnley, the amateur architect whose extraordinary manuscript *Miscelanea Structura Curiosa* of 1745 still survives in the library at Birr. His eccentric designs of grottoes, cascades, fountains, obelisks, garden buildings, Palladian villas, and public buildings seem never to have been executed; his only extant work is a Doric column in the main square of Birr.

Sir Laurence's grandson, another Laurence, 2nd Earl of Rosse, was a patriotic politician and a friend of statesmen Edmund Burke and Henry Flood, the leader of the Patriot Party. As his sketchbook reveals, he remodeled the castle in the early nineteenth century with the help of the architect John Johnston. The most notable addition was the great Gothic music room. With its web of Gothic plaster vaulting and huge tracery windows picked out in white and gold, looking down onto the tumbling falls of the River Camcor, this is one of the most theatrical rooms in Ireland. The whole composition brings to mind Horace Walpole's Gothic Revival villa, Strawberry Hill. The exterior of the castle was cloaked with a Gothic mantel with stepped battlements and a huge arched recessed entrance with flanking coats of arms and arrow loops.

The most important episode in the history of Birr took place in the mid-nineteenth century with the reign of the 2nd Earl's son, William, 3rd Earl of Rosse, who was educated at home by his father until he went to university. His fame lies in his scientific interests (he was president of the Royal Society), particularly in the field of astronomy. In the grounds of Birr, he erected what was for many years the largest telescope in the world, which brought visitors from all over the world

ABOVE: *The Leviathan of Parsonstown: when it was erected by the 3rd Earl of Rosse it was the largest telescope in the world.*

OPPOSITE: *View of an allée in the walled garden. The gardens at Birr are among the most famous in Ireland.*

PRECEDING PAGE LEFT: *Two photographs of Maud Messel, daughter of the cartoonist Edward Linley Sambourne, on the desk in the Gothic music room. One shows her with her two children, Oliver, the stage designer, and Anne, who married the 6th Earl of Rosse.*

PRECEDING PAGE RIGHT: *Detail of an eighteenth-century giltwood mirror reflecting the ribbed vaulting of the Gothic music room.*

to see the Leviathan of Parsonstown. Caroline Fox, the English Quaker intellectual and a contemporary visitor, wrote in a letter dated September 16, 1852:

Parsonstown was our first stopping-place, and there we had a really sublime treat in seeing Lord Rosse's telescopes, listening to his admirable explanations and histories of his experiences, watching his honest manly face, seeing the drawings of nebulae and the cast of a lunar crater, which are the cherished pets of Lady Rosse, and finally being called from our coffee by the advent of a double star on a hazy night. These we watched through the three and a half foot telescope, and rejoiced in their contrasted colors of blue and yellow. Then through the monster (in the tube of which we all promenaded at once) we gazed at some groups of stars, but the moon, alas! was impenetrably veiled. The easy yet solemn movements of the vast machine, just visible in the starlight, was in itself a grand sight, quite poetical, even independently of its high purpose.

The 3rd Earl's wife, Mary, Countess of Rosse was an accomplished pioneering photographer. Her dark room still survives, complete with everything from chemicals to blackout shutters. She was the subject of a fascinating recent exhibition at Birr showing many of her photographs. Not surprisingly, their children were just as talented: the eldest son, Lawrence, who became the 4th Earl of Rosse, continued in his father's footsteps, while the youngest son, Sir Charles Parsons, was the inventor of the steam turbine. His prototype vessel, the *Turbinia*, caused a sensation at the naval review for Queen Victoria's Diamond Jubilee in 1897 and led to the adoption of the steam turbine for the propulsion of ships, which ultimately transformed the fleets of the world.

The next generation was blighted by the tragic death of William Parsons, the 5th Earl

who died of wounds received in World War I. His son, Lawrence, the 6th Earl, succeeded as a minor and was one of the Bright Young Things, a group of aristocrats and bohemians at Oxford in the 1920s. He married Anne Messel, the sister of the painter and designer Oliver Messel. The Rosses became prominent in horticultural and conservationist circles in Ireland and England and were friends of numerous figures in the art and literary world, including Harold Acton, John Betjeman, Robert Byron, and James Lees-Milne. Birr Castle was dashingly done up by Anne Rosse and the park became one of the greatest arboretums in Ireland. She and her husband were great hosts, Anne Rosse recalled: "We did not entertain every weekend. For me it was always much easier to have a big party than several small ones, because you're giving out less in a kind of a way. At Birr we've had seventy-eight sitting down for luncheon—always sit-down. If people have come to see a big garden, they long to sit down." She continued describing the routine of the household there:

There were still, when I went to Birr, for each day, six different lunches in six different rooms. The staff could on occasion meet and talk together—Nanny could gossip with the housekeeper in the housekeeper's room, or Miss Martin the governess could gossip with Nanny either in the schoolroom or the nursery. But eating together—NO. Naturally the housekeeper was permanently at war with the cook and her staff. The darling butler and his staff had a wing and a world of their own. The

RIGHT: *Developing chemicals that belonged to Mary, Countess of Rosse, have remained on the shelves of her darkroom since the 1850s.*

OPPOSITE: *Steps wind down to the wine cellar in the depths of the original castle.*

OVERLEAF: *Anne, Countess of Rosse; created the yellow drawing room from two rooms, a renovation that nearly brought the entire ceiling crashing down.*

PAGES 28–29: *The Conroy room, filled with family memorabilia and named after Sir Edward Conroy, Baronet, who eloped with Alicia Parsons, daughter of the 2nd Earl of Rosse, in 1837.*

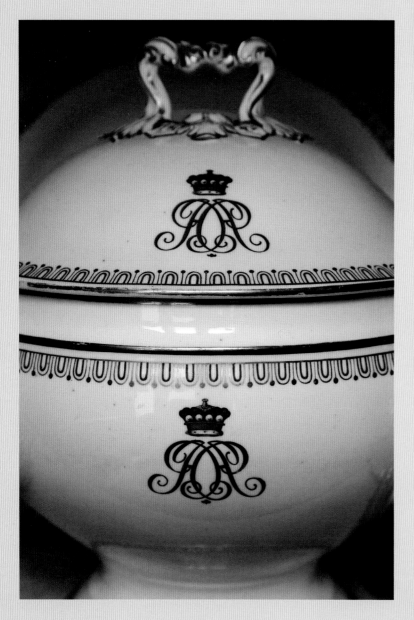

Monogrammed family china fills a glazed cabinet in the corridor outside the dining room.

OPPOSITE: *An illuminated manuscript on vellum in the muniments room, decorated with the Parsons coat of arms.*

I remember once a member of the Royal Family came to stay. The house was very full. Suddenly, at about three in the morning, there was a little tap at the door, and there were two little people with their suitcases, saying the house was on fire. Oh dear, oh dear, what had happened? In fact, the central heating had got so hot that the wallpaper had peeled off and fallen over the four-poster bed. Poor things, they thought it was the house on fire. It was just one of those things that happens in an Irish house.

Anne Rosse's son Brendan, the present earl, and his wife, Alison, have continued in the distinguished footsteps of the family. They have created the Birr Scientific and Heritage Foundation, housed in the former stable block, and the archive has been calendared and regularized and is now possibly the only family-operated archive service in Ireland. Scholars from all over the world visit these resources. Brendan continues with the planting tradition of his family by going on expeditions and bringing back seeds and specimens from the Far East and central Asia, which ensures the continued development of a magic demesne.

lady of the house soon learnt her round. Down first to the housekeeper's room. She would invariably ask me how many guests and when and who. Then to the kitchen to give orders to the farm that week. Then to the darling pantry boys, to tell them what sort of guests and what silver and china to put out.

Her son from her first marriage, Anthony Armstrong-Jones, the famous photographer, married Princess Margaret in 1960, which led to royal visits. She recalled one of these visits:

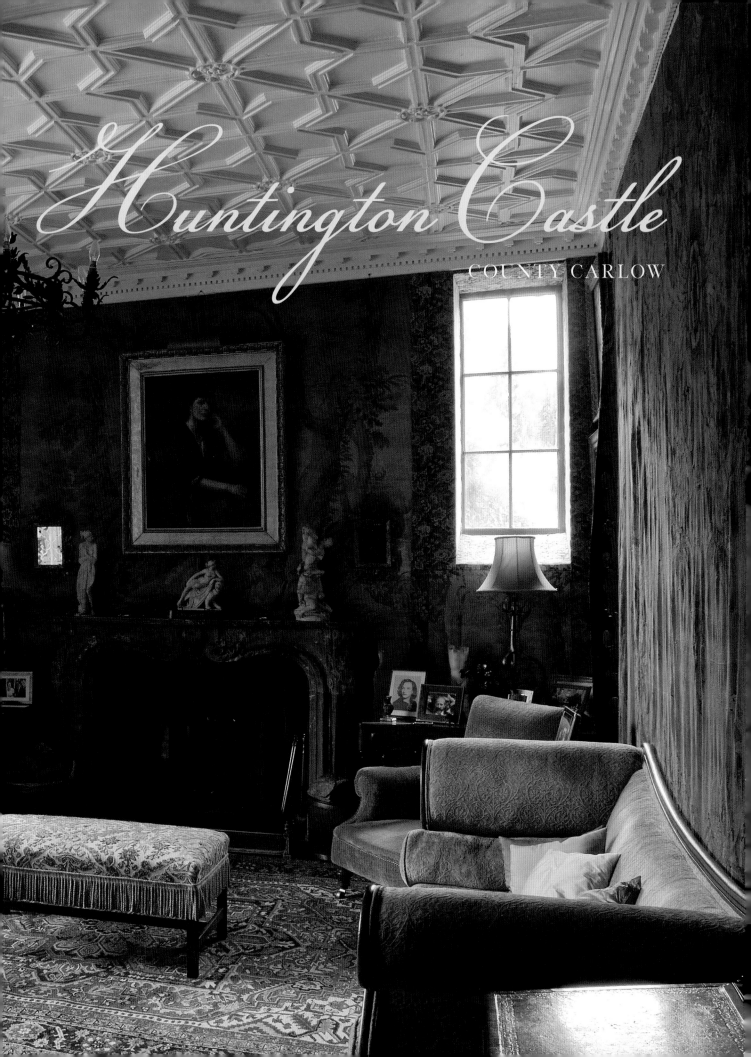

Huntington Castle

COUNTY CARLOW

The higgledy-piggledy nature of the rooms continues upstairs with odd staircases rising in short flights, creaking corridor floorboards, and new bathrooms hidden in former closets. One door opens into a library with books and old photograph albums strewn about the floor.

Tucked off the main street of Clonegal, a discreet gatehouse and pair of iron gates mark the start of a navelike avenue of majestic lime trees ending in the ancient fortress of the Esmonde family, Huntington Castle, its crenellated outline topped by a fluttering flag. The passage of time is evident in the wear on the mossy stones and the overgrown plantings; events here stretch far back into the annals of history, where fact becomes entwined with myth and legend. Set against the picturesque backdrop of the

Blackstairs Mountains, near the convergence of the Slaney and Derry rivers, it is obvious why Franciscan monks established a priory here in the thirteenth century.

Early in the fifteenth century, a granite keep was built on the site. It later passed into the hands of the Netterville family, who in turn sold it to Sir Laurence Esmonde in the early seventeenth century. Sir Laurence was an ambitious soldier who left behind his Catholic origins and converted to Protestantism, swearing

Traces of the late-seventeenth-century formal gardens can still be seen in the lime avenue (above) and yew walks.

OPPOSITE: *A staircase on one of the upper floors.*

PRECEDING PAGES: *Aubusson tapestries line the walls of the room leading to the conservatory.*

A photograph of the yew avenue in an old family album shows how little it has changed over the last hundred years.

BELOW: *African hunting trophies line the walls of the hall.*

OPPOSITE: *The entrance hall's eclectic chimneypiece has a baroque-influenced relief (see detail) and mediavalizing tower piers, which echo Huntington's crenellated roofline.*

allegiance to Elizabeth I and later receiving a knighthood. In 1622, as major-general of James I's forces in Ireland and governor of Duncannon Fort, he was raised to the peerage, becoming Lord Esmonde. Three years later, he built a tower house on the site of the earlier keep and this forms the nucleus of the present-day castle. Despite his Protestant leanings, Sir Laurence married Ailish O'Flaherty, a devout Catholic and granddaughter of Grace O'Malley, the pirate queen. This clash of religious leanings resulted in the abduction of their son Thomas, by Grace, to her family in Connaught, so he could be brought up a Catholic. The episode seems not to have been of undue concern to Sir Laurence, for he found himself another wife, this time a Protestant.

Sir Laurence's abducted son and heir died shortly after his father, so Huntington passed to his grandson, Sir Laurence Esmonde, 2nd Baronet. In the 1680s, he made the castle more domestic and was likely responsible for the formal gardens, whose rigid linear planning is still apparent in places such as the lime avenue. A ghostly avenue of 120 English yew trees with long trailing branches arching like tentacles over the path is no doubt part of this early garden scheme. A wing was added to the castle about 1720, and further alterations were carried out in the 1860s by Alexander Durdin, whose uncle had married the Esmonde daughters of the 5th and 7th Baronets, respectively. His daughter, Helen, inherited Huntington and married Herbert Robertson, a member of parliament for South Hackney. In the

mid-1890s, the Robertsons added the picturesque battlemented range to the back of the castle overlooking the yard. Their son, Manning Durdin-Robertson, was an architect and thus could not resist further meddling with the castle.

The result of all of these alterations is a marvelous hotchpotch of rooms and decoration. The present entrance hall, reached from the shelter of the courtyard at the back of the castle, has an eclectic display of hunting trophies brought back from African adventures by the intrepid Nora Parsons, wife of Manning Durdin-Robertson. An Italian old-master painting of the Archangel Michael triumphant over the devil hangs in an elaborate

pierced gilded frame above a castellated oak chimneypiece. This room leads up a flight of steps to the original hall, now used as a dining room, its walls hung with Bedouin tent hangings brought back by Herbert Robertson from a tour of Tunisia in the 1870s. The large stone fireplace is dated 1625 on the keystone, while the stained glass window nearby proudly proclaims the Esmonde genealogy. These, together with the early family portraits ranged on the walls below the Jacobethan plasterwork ceiling, give the room a distinctly otherworldly feel.

More family portraits, with gilded frames reflected in old looking glasses, line the dark oak-paneled passageways. One depicts Anne Penn, the third wife of an earlier Alexander Durdin (who married four times), through whom the family inherited vast estates in Pennsylvania in 1767, later lost in the Revolutionary War. Today, the family uses what is known as the tapestry room to relax and unwind. A French note is added to the decoration with a large Louis XV–style marble chimneypiece and nineteenth-century Aubusson tapestries lining the

HELEN wife of ARUNDEL HILL.
daughter of Garret Nagle & maternal
great grandmother of Herbert Robertson
B. 1752 — D. 1830.

1625

ABOVE AND RIGHT:
*Old family photograph
albums and estate maps can
be found in the library.*

OPPOSITE: *A nineteenth-
century marble beauty
stands on the mantelpiece
in the tapestry room.*

OVERLEAF: *Flights of
stairs rise and descend
in all shapes and sizes at
Huntington.*

walls. Nora Parsons's portrait hangs
above, although it is a rather more wistful
portrayal of the authoress than one might
have supposed from her passion for blood
sports. Across the room from Nora's portrait
hangs a painting of the Slaney Valley from
Huntington by the English landscape painter
Cecil Gordon Lawson. The artist was in love
with Nora, but when she refused his hand in
marriage, he left the castle dejected and his
painting unfinished.

In the 1930s, the children of the
castle painted a charming naive mural of
their home on the wall of the Victorian
conservatory. It complements the sculpture
of a man by David Durdin-Robertson that
sits nearby. The vine, which forms a green

canopy over the room, was grown from a cutting taken in the 1860s from the famous Great Vine at Hampton Court.

The higgledy-piggledy nature of the rooms continues upstairs with odd staircases rising in short flights, creaking corridor floorboards, and new bathrooms tucked away in former closets. One door opens into a library with books and old photograph albums strewn about the floor. Another opens into a freshly painted bedroom, the mahogany four-post bed hung with crewelwork while the walls are decorated with watercolors by Robert Manning, a travel companion of J. M. W. Turner. It is among these rooms that a priest's hole, a secret hiding place for Catholic priests, was discovered, sealed up with a candle and spoon inside.

At the top of the house, lies the studio of the current owner, Moira Durdin-Robertson. It is here, hidden away in the former attics, that Moira (née McCaffery) finds the peace and quiet to paint, atop the layers of history that fill the space beneath her.

OPPOSITE: *Old photograph albums and schoolbooks are among the ephemera found on the shelves in the library.*

OVERLEAF: *Bishop Leslie's Room, named after the eighteenth-century bishop of Limerick, whose ghost is said to stand at the foot of the bed or appear in a ghostly portrait over the mantelpiece.*

PAGES 50–51: *The lush conservatory is approached through a Gothic arched doorway in the tapestry room.*

Burtown House

COUNTY KILDARE

*O*ur eyes were charmed with the sweetest bottom where, through lofty trees, we beheld a variety of pleasant dwellings. Through a road that looked like a fine terrace walk, we turn to this lovely vale, where Nature assisted by Art gave us the utmost contentment.

Throughout Ireland, small Georgian country houses of pleasing proportions are often encompassed by a picturesque park with venerable oaks and beech trees. However, it is rare to find one of these houses still in the possession of the family that built it. Burtown is one of these treasures, passed down through the generations and still very much a family home. Though not as grand as some country houses, Burtown is an important example of a modest country house. The small size may have helped save it from the burnings of so many of the great houses of Ireland that took place during the Civil War of 1920–23.

Burtown House was built about 1710 by the Quaker Robert Power; the house is marked on early maps as Power's Grove. Originally only one room deep, wings were soon added; only their faint outlines remain. In

the late eighteenth century, the house was enlarged with the addition of a bow-fronted room on the garden front with a bedroom above and a grand staircase lit by a tall, rounded-arch sash window. Pretty plasterwork was also introduced at this time, most notably in an arched alcove in the bow-fronted room, which is filled with a shallow fan and delightful sprays of grapevine flanked by a pair of classical vases surmounting pilasters composed with foliage and naive Corinthian capitals.

ABOVE: *Burtown is surrounded by Lesley Fennell's lush gardens.*

LEFT: *A plaster bust in the hall looks out into the park through the Georgian fanlight.*

OPPOSITE: *A plasterwork urn on the alcove in the drawing room.*

PRECEDING PAGES: *The garden front of Burtown glimpsed through the early morning mist.*

OVERLEAF: *The bow-fronted drawing room was added in the late eighteenth century.*

This room was probably the dining room and the sideboard would have fit into the alcove; the presence of the grape leaves would support this theory, as they are the symbol of Bacchus, Roman god of wine and festivity. Members of the Irish squirearchy were well known for their hospitality and the dining room was often the largest room in the house. Bishop George Berkeley, the philosopher, eminent divine, and well-traveled man of letters and taste, wrote in the early eighteenth century: "The whole Business of the Day is to course down a Hare or some other such worthy Purchase; to get over a most enormous and immoderate Dinner; and guzzle down a proportionable quantity of Wine."

A later inhabitant of Burtown, William James Fennell (1866–1928), who was a keen horseman, was "asked to leave the Quaker persuasion because of his fondness for driving a carriage with uniformed flunkeys on the back," which suggests that the family was retreating from its puritanical Quaker origins.

Elliptical arches decorated with borders of foliage mark the openings to the staircase, and more delicate plasterwork decorates the ceiling. The hall

PRECEDING PAGE LEFT:
The top of the staircase has a pretty plasterwork ceiling.

PRECEDING PAGE RIGHT:
A plaster bust in the entry hall.

CLOCKWISE FROM TOP LEFT:
A silver salver in the hall. Detail of a Georgian wardrobe. Engraved glass decanters in a bedroom. A Victorian chair in the master bedroom. Lesley Fennell's engagement photograph and wedding photograph. William Fennell's racing binoculars with Punchestown Races badges.

ABOVE AND DETAILS: *An ornate Italian-style dressing table in the master bedroom.*

OPPOSITE: *William Fennell and his wife, Isabel Shackleton, dressed in hunting habit.*

ceiling has plasterwork in the manner of James Wyatt, with neoclassical swags and medallions. Each of the four corners of the room is quirkily mounted with a classical bust on a bracket.

Like many Irish houses, Burtown passed through the female line, from the Powers to the Houghtons to the Wakefields; the latter inheriting it in the early nineteenth century. During the Wakefields' tenure the front of the house was given a facelift with a fanlighted entrance door, recessed in an arch, enlarged sash windows, and a roof with deep eaves. When Mr. Wakefield was

killed by a cricket ball, the house passed to his sister Jemima, wife of James Fennell (1817–1890). James was descended from Colonel John Fennell (1626–1706), an English officer in Oliver Cromwell's army who was granted a small estate on the banks of the River Suir outside Cahir, Co. Tipperary. He later became a Quaker, at a time when Quakerism was increasing in popularity and sweeping across the British Isles. Burtown is close to the village of Ballitore, one of Ireland's most prominent Quaker strongholds. The former Ballitore Boarding School

ABOVE AND OPPOSITE:
The staircase added in the late eighteenth century.

BELOW: *Detail of the staircase's foliate decoration.*

OVERLEAF: *The dining room is in the original part of the house.*

was founded in 1726 by the Yorkshire-born Quaker Abraham Shackleton, with pupils attending from as far away as France, Norway, and Jamaica. Its most famous pupil was Edmund Burke, the philosopher and statesman. In 1748, an English traveler visited Ballitore and wrote: "Our eyes were charmed with the sweetest bottom where, through lofty trees, we beheld a variety of pleasant dwellings. Through a road that looked like a fine terrace walk, we turn to this lovely vale, where Nature assisted by Art gave us the utmost contentment. It is a colony of Quakers, called by the name of Ballitore."

James and Jemima's son, William James Fennell was a keen horseman, a passion that has continued in the family to the present day. He married Isabel Shackleton, cousin of the famous Antarctic explorer Sir Ernest Shackleton. William and Isabel's son, Jim, an officer in the Royal Artillery, inherited Burtown and lived there until 1963, when his son, William, took over.

Artistic genes abound in the house: Burtown is now home to William's widow, Lesley Fennell, an accomplished artist, who lives in the main house and has transformed the house's gardens. The walls are hung with her work, including portraits of various members of the family. Her son, James, and his wife, Joanna, and their children live in one half of the old stable block, while Lesley's mother, the botanical artist Wendy Walsh, lives in the other half. James is a well-known photographer (and photographer of this book), and Joanna is a jewelry designer.

Kilruddery

COUNTY WICKLOW

*T*he result was an enormous many-gabled mansion, which ornamented the skyline with pepper pot chimneys, balustrades, crenellation and an ogee dome on the turreted entrance. It cost a staggering 20,000 pounds excluding the cost of furniture and marbles from France and Italy.

An extraordinary primitive painting from the 1740s, now hanging in Killruddery's library, shows a glimpse of how the house once looked. It depicts the Killruddery hunt: hounds, horsemen, and riders, in decoupage, galloping over the Wicklow landscape with the Sugarloaf Mountain looming in the background. A famous poem by Thomas Mozeen describes the Killruddery hunt:

In Seventeen Hundred and Forty and Four,
The fifth of December, I think 'twas no more,
At five in the morning by most of the clocks,
We rode from Killruddery in search of a fox.

The house shown in the painting faces east and a circular carriage sweep leads up to the relatively plain twin-gabled house topped by a cupola. To the south of the house, the straight sides of two long canals can be seen, which together with the *pattes-d'oie* ("goose feet," the intersecting garden paths known as the Angles) form part of one of the most complete Baroque gardens to survive in the British Isles. The gardens were laid out by a French designer named Bonnet in 1682, a disciple of the famous André le Nôtre, designer of the gardens at Versailles.

Killruddery was leased by its owners, the Brabazon family, Earls of Meath, in 1711, and the advertisement in *The Dublin Intelligencer* for April 14 of that year, described it as: "a large house with 4 Flankers and Terris, and a new Summer-House built by the late Earl, with 4 Rooms on a Floor well Wainscotted, and in

TOP: *The conservatory is used as a sculpture gallery to house the marbles collected by the 10th Earl of Meath on his Grand Tour in 1816–17.*

ABOVE: *The south and east elevation in 1886, before the house was reduced in size in the mid-twentieth century.*

OPPOSITE: *A bronze statue in the Angles, a formal Baroque planting of yew, hornbeam, and lime.*

PRECEDING PAGES: *Detail of a painting with a view of Killruddery, c. 1740, with decoupage horses and hounds.*

good Order, with Pleasure Garden," and goes on to describe the bowling green, gravel walks, fish ponds, and offices (including stables, dairy, and kennels). The Sylvan Theater, used for outdoor theatricals, and the Beech Circle, composed of a round pond surrounded by 30-foot hedges interspersed with statues, were probably planted at a later date. The interior of the beech hedges was originally cut with ornamental niches nearly 20 feet high. The pond is centered by a jet of water and four spouting stone cherubs; the jet enlivens the still water and contrasts the greenery of the beech hedges. The garden feels like that of a Hubert Robert romantic painting or a Florentine villa. At the end of the main vista a double avenue of lime trees crosses the park. An old plan of the demesne from the 1740s shows a further canal and radiating avenues, which have since disappeared.

Due to the disrupted succession of the Earls of Meath, the gardens remained relatively unscathed during the eighteenth

century, while those of other houses were swept away. Fortunately, the tenure of the 10th and 11th Earls coincided with a revived appreciation for formality in gardening. John Chambre Brabazon, the 10th Earl, a man of great taste, employed the architect Daniel Robertson to restore the gardens and lay out the lower parterre in 1846. Sir George Hodson, a neighbor and amateur architect, designed the charming ornamental dairy in the fashionable picturesque style as popularized by Humphrey Repton.

The 10th Earl took his Grand Tour in Italy in 1816–17, and there ordered marbles and chimneypieces mainly through Gaspare Gabrielli, a painter who had worked in Ireland decorating the drawing room at Lyons, Co. Kildare with landscapes inspired by Claude Lorraine. Soon after the Earl returned to Ireland, he employed the father and son architects Richard and William Vitruvius Morrison to rebuild the house in the neo-Tudor style. The result was an enormous multi-gabled mansion that ornamented the skyline with pepper-pot chimneys, balustrades, crenellation, and an ogee dome on the turreted entrance. It cost a staggering 20,000 pounds, excluding the cost of furniture and marbles from France and Italy.

The genius of the Morrisons is clearly seen in the design and use of space in the two drawing rooms on the south front;

OPPOSITE AND RIGHT:
The dining room with its classicizing stuccoed ceiling and chimneypiece by Giacinto Micali was originally designed as another drawing room. The portrait over the sideboard depicts the 14th Earl of Meath as a young officer in the Grenadier Guards.

OVERLEAF: *The sculpture gallery includes work by Bertel Thorwaldsen and Joseph Nollekens, whose bust of William Pitt is displayed on a marble column.*

here they rejected the neo-Tudor style in favor of neoclassicism probably influenced by Giacinto Micali's chimneypiece, ordered through the good offices of Gabrielli in Italy in 1817. The influx of eighteenth-century French furniture in Ireland influenced the designs of Matthew Wyatt, Jr., for Louis Revival wall panels and elaborate pelmet cornices, some of which survive, and were probably executed by James Del Vecchio in Dublin. Each room has an elaborate plasterwork ceiling executed by the local stuccodore Henry Pobje. The late Betty, Countess of Meath discovered a signature dated April 24, 1824 when she was painting the ceiling of the large drawing room herself. This room has four green Ionic scagliola columns screening either end. The smaller of the two rooms, now used as a dining room, has a shallow domed ceiling in the manner of Percier and Fontaine, with a geometric laurel design and floral garlands with doves; feigned drapery fills the lunettes. Beyond the present dining room is the dramatic sculpture gallery, designed in 1852 by William Burn as a conservatory to house the marbles collected by the 10th Earl on his Grand Tour. The pierced parapet is traditionally said to have been based on Lady Meath's tiara—which was sold in order to pay for it.

The enormous Tudor Revival pile was found to have a serious attack of dry rot in the early 1950s that necessitated the demolition of a third of the house. The architect Claud Phillimore was responsible

RIGHT AND FAR RIGHT:
The staircase hall was originally much larger until the house was reduced in size in the 1950s.

OPPOSITE: *A stained-glass window is reflected in an eighteenth-century Irish-giltwood pier glass.*

OVERLEAF: *Threadbare floral chintz barely covers a Georgian sofa in the south bedroom. A portrait of Mary, Countess of Meath (wife of the 12th Earl) and her dog hangs in the east bedroom.*

for the remodeling, including reducing the grand double ramp staircase to two flights, thus giving a clearer view of the mid-nineteenth-century Gothic stained glass window. The window depicts the arrival of William the Conqueror to England in 1066, with his standard-bearer Jacques le Brabacon, traditionally the ancestor of the Brabazons.

Jacques's descendant, the 10th Earl, clearly had a military bearing as when the writer Sir Walter Scott met him in 1827 while staying with friends in Ayrshire, Scott wrote in his Journal that "the resemblance between the Earl of Meath and the Duke of Wellington is something remarkably striking–it is not only the profile, but the mode of bearing the person, and the person itself. Lady Theodora, the Earl's daughter, and a beautiful young lady, told me that in Paris her father was often taken for Lord Wellington."

The present Earl of Meath, known as Jack, is passionate about gardening and has done much to restore both the house and gardens over the last decade, together with his wife, Xenia. Their son, Anthony Jacques, is in the process of taking over the management of Killruddery. The house is now frequently used for events and films, most recently *The Tudors*, so visitors can easily find themselves strolling through the Angles into the midst of a costume drama.

Tarbert House

COUNTY KERRY

*L*ady Portarlington, who thought the Leslies "trumpery people," visited Tarbert on her way to Killarney in 1784 and avoided the family but looked with admiration over the beautiful demesne with its river views. She finished her description of the woods: "but I am sorry to say he is cutting a great deal of it down, for which he deserves to have his head cut off."

As the great River Shannon moves its way toward the sea, the estuary is interrupted by a slip of wooded land leading to a lighthouse built in the 1830s. These woods encircle the house of the Leslie family of Tarbert. The industrial world has invaded this romantic view with the great stacks of the Tarbert power station (which replaced a Napoleonic fort) dominating the skyline.

The Leslies, who settled here in 1690 after the Williamite War, were descended from the Lords of Rothes, a noble Scottish family in turn descended from the Hungarian family of L'Essele, descended, so it was said, from Attila the Hun. The Leslies produced many bishops and churchmen among their ranks and are related to the Leslies of Glasslough, Co. Monoghan, another well-known ascendancy family. James Leslie, Bishop of Limerick assumed his miter in 1755. He was chosen because of his knowledge of his native Kerry. Tradition in the family held that he built his new house in the center of the diocese, midway between Limerick

and Killarney. He also bought Huntington Castle in Co. Carlow (another chapter in this book). Dean Jonathan Swift, a noted cleric of the eighteenth century, quipped about the family: "The Leslies have lots of books upon their shelves, / All written by Leslies about themselves."

Tarbert House is a simple classical box typical of eighteenth-century Irish country houses. Originally it had two floors of seven bays with a high roof and three dormer windows on each face. The present third floor was created later in the century and both facades of the house are shown in a

ABOVE: *A pen-and-ink drawing of Robert Leslie by Colonel Park, c. 1850, with Tarbert House in the background.*

OPPOSITE: *Steps lead from French doors in the present dining room into the garden.*

PRECEDING PAGES: *A bayonet holder in the hall, c. 1798, decorated with the Leslie crest and buckle badge surmounted by an Irish harp and the Royal crown.*

OVERLEAF: *The north front of Tarbert, facing toward the river Shannon, viewed from across the park.*

pair of watercolors dating from 1795 by the English artist John Charles Barrow. The plan of the house is straightforward, with a central spine wall that services all the chimneys, four reception rooms leading off the front hall, and a single staircase from basement to attic. A more spacious staircase was created to the left of the hall in the late eighteenth century and has some rudimentary neoclassical plasterwork. The hall and library still have the original variegated marble Georgian mantelpieces set almost flush against the wall, however the most interesting room in the house is the finely paneled library with its pair of Ionic pilasters flanking the marble mantelpiece. Inside a cupboard, in the paneling in a corner of the room, some of the original olive green paint was discovered, although the room has since been painted in lighter shades of yellow. The floor of the room has its original herringbone parquet floor and the hall next door has black and white painted tiles.

The house stands on a large basement, with some vaulted rooms. A wine cellar with original bins takes up one corner, while the east end is dominated by a capacious kitchen with hooks for smoking salmon out of the Shannon, an early-nineteenth-century Cork manufactured range, and an oven unused for fifty years. A door leads out to a courtyard and further offices, which once would have bustled with life and now lie deserted.

The north front of the house, which looks down to the Shannon, is centered by a

ABOVE AND RIGHT: The staircase was added in the late eighteenth century.

OPPOSITE: The library viewed from the hall.

OVERLEAF LEFT: A family photograph album (from the Collis-Sandes family) sits across a handwritten journal with the "Standing Orders for the Moveable Column of the Peshawur Force," a relic of the days of the Raj.

OVERLEAF RIGHT: Porcelain figures adorn the drawing room.

well-proportioned cut-stone door case with a straight entablature. Clearly there was an earlier house at Tarbert, but the simple plan suggests that the present building does not incorporate any previous house. In the Barrow watercolors, an older gabled building is clearly visible and this could have been the residence of the bishop's father and grandfather. Charles Smith in his 1756 *History of Kerry*, wrote that the house was "finely situated, and commanded an extensive view of the river Shannon" and continued that the estate and mansion now belonged to the bishop. All the detailing of Tarbert appears to date from the mid-eighteenth century and the house is one of the very few of this period to survive in County Kerry and one of the only ones with the original family still living in it. Two portraits of the bishop in his lawn sleeves hang in the hall. The smaller one belongs to a series of four portraits of the bishop, his eldest son, and two brothers painted by the well-known mid-eighteenth century Irish artist Philip Hussey.

Bishop Leslie had a large family of two sons and eight daughters. His son Edward is shown in a portrait hanging over the mantelpiece in the library as a handsome young blade in a blue and gold braided coat. The bishop died in 1770 and Edward took over running the estate. By 1773 *The Limerick Chronicle* advertised the leasing of lands "for such terms, years or lives as may be agreed." In 1772 the See house in Limerick, the bishop's official residence, was to be sold. In 1774, Edward was laying out a

village on his Tarbert lands and looking for artificers to work there. It was Edward who added the third story to the house and incorporated the new staircase.

Edward was an Irish Member of Parliament and had an active military career in the Irish Volunteers (a military organization formed to defend the country from foreign invasion when British soldiers were fighting in the American Revolutionary War) between 1779 and 1780

ABOVE: *The Irish mahogany table and chairs in the hall are probably original to the house.*

OPPOSITE: *Bishop James Leslie, a former owner of Tarbert House, in a mid-eighteenth-century portrait by Irish artist Philip Hussey.*

OVERLEAF: *The gun racks flanking the portraits and the bayonet holders above the doors were used when Sir Edward Leslie, 1st Baronet, raised the Loyal Tarbert Regiment of Fencibles in the 1780s.*

and raised the Loyal Tarbert Regiment of Fencibles (a temporary army unit composed of volunteers for patrolling local areas). Telling relics of those days are the original gun racks in the front hall and carved wooden bayonet holders with the Leslie thistle crest and the buckles with the coat of arms over each of the four doors. Arched elements secure the bayonets, which would have made a decorative fan, also seen at Glin Castle.

Edward was made a baronet in 1787. Lady Portarlington, who thought the Leslies "trumpery people," visited Tarbert on her way to Killarney in 1784 and avoided the family but looked with admiration over the beautiful demesne with its river views. She finished her description of the woods: "but I am sorry to say he is cutting a great deal of it down, for which he deserves to have his head cut off." He needed to raise money for election expenses. (Edward was described by Lord Kenmare in 1795 at the time of a county election as: "the most long winded tiresome bore.") However, since Sir Edward had no son to inherit the estate (it was entailed to his cousin Robert), he continued cutting down the woods, though it was illegal. Fortunately, many fine trees have grown to cover the estate today.

Ursula Leslie, who lives at Tarbert today, says there are still letters in the house from the famous Irish politician Daniel O'Connell dealing with the complications of the estate's inheritance. By 1878 the property consisted

of 1,747 acres. In 1903 Major Cecil Leslie sold all the outlying farms. However, he kept the fishing rights, in true Irish tradition, although they finally had to be sold in 1969 when the power station was built. Its ever-looming presence is a reminder of the twenty-first century outside the circlet of woods that preserve the old-fashioned atmosphere of this charming house.

TOP: *Millicent Leslie lived in Tarbert House in the Victorian era.*

ABOVE: *Amateur dramatics being performed by Victorian members of the Collis-Sandes family, relations of the Leslies.*

OPPOSITE: *A photograph of Cecil Leslie (1874–1953) as a young officer in the Royal Munster Fusiliers on top of a military notebook for the Kerry Militia dated 1856.*

Glin Castle

COUNTY LIMERICK

John Fraunceis changed the name from Glin House to Glin Castle in keeping with its new status. This would be typical of the romantic notions of the 1820s—he obviously thought that the holder of such an ancient title should be living in a castle like his medieval ancestors.

The romantically titled Knights of Glin, a branch of the great Norman family the FitzGeralds or Geraldines, Earls of Desmond, were granted extensive lands in Co. Limerick in the early fourteenth century by their Desmond overlords.

The old Glin Castle was the subject of a dramatic siege in 1600 by Queen Elizabeth's forces and the Knight's lands were confiscated. Before the siege Sir George Carew, the Lord President of Munster, captured the Knight's six-year-old son and, tying the child to the mouth of a cannon, threatened to blow him to bits if the Knight did not surrender. The reply, in Irish, was blunt: the Knight was virile and his wife was strong and it would be easy to produce another son.

In 1615 the family was back in the castle and an inscription on a mantelpiece, now mounted above the entrance gates to the present courtyard, commemorates the restoration of their lands. The mid-seventeenth century saw another siege at Glin during the English Civil War and by the late seventeenth century they had removed west to a thatched long house, which is

incorporated into the wing of the present castle. In the first half of the eighteenth century, it is probable that the wing was turned into a T-shape with an extension facing east and some large double-height rooms. This is the only way they could have fit the full-length portrait of John FitzGerald, by a Dutch artist. He was a famous duelist and is depicted with his servant accepting a challenge.

The painting now hangs in the front hall, which was part of the next phase of building, carried out in the 1790s by John FitzGerald's nephew, another John. He created the hall with Corinthian columns and an elaborate neoclassical plasterwork ceiling leading on to the unique feature of the house: the double-ramped bifurcated staircase, which rises to the bedroom floor. The drawing room and the library, also with fine plasterwork, were part of this extension to the house. Also added was

ABOVE: *Detail of the FitzGerald coat of arms on the hall ceiling.*

OPPOSITE: *A Palladian window on the staircase looks onto the garden.*

PRECEDING PAGES: *The miniature fort on the banks of the Shannon was originally designed as a bathing house for changing before swimming.*

OVERLEAF: *The gardens on the south front are a riot of color in spring.*

a Palladian window on the south front, halfway up the stairs, decorated with charming high-relief Rococo cornucopias, looking onto the garden. The library has a superbly crafted broken-pediment bookcase set into the wall, with a hidden door concealed behind the oval trellis with the remains of crimson backing silk.

The hall (below), with its Corinthian columns and elaborate plaster ceiling (right), was added in the 1790s. Above the doors in the hall are bayonet racks dating from the 1780s. The portrait (opposite) by Heroman van der Mijn, c. 1740, shows the 20th Knight of Glin being handed a challenge to a duel.

OVERLEAF LEFT:
Cantonese porcelain is reflected in a mirror on the staircase landing.

OVERLEAF RIGHT:
The staircase begins as two flights and then joins to continue as one.

What was the cause of this sophisticated series of rooms built in the wilds of west Limerick in the 1790s, which tell a tale of taste and enlightenment? The earlier FitzGeralds, in their thatched long house and fairly modest extension, were best represented by a rather wild, horse-loving and smuggling series of four Knights of Glin, all brothers, better known for their lives of debt and debauchery, than for a love of architecture and decoration. The reason for the sudden refinement was the 1789 marriage of Colonel John FitzGerald, an ardent volunteer and militiaman, to Margaretta Maria Fraunceis, the daughter of a rich West Country squire who owned Forde Abbey in Dorset, Combe Florey in Somerset, and other manor houses in Devon and Glamorganshire. Glin, with its relatively humble living quarters, must have seemed a far cry from the superb Stuart interiors of Forde Abbey, with its carved staircases and salon hung with a set of magnificent Mortlake tapestries after Raphael, and from Combe Florey, with its elegant Georgian reception rooms and Gibbsian rusticated facade.

Margaretta's marriage settlement maddeningly went unrecorded, but as Colonel John inherited a sea of debts from his rackety uncles, it must have been considerable and certainly paid for much of the building work. Margaretta's coat of arms is impaled with John's on the

hall ceiling. The decoration of the hall's plasterwork symbolized the martial spirit of the age with military trophies: Roman peltae (small shields) sprouting shamrocks underlined patriotic feelings and oval plaques on the ceiling represented Peace, Justice, and War. Previously thought to date from the early 1780s, more recent scholarship dates the ceiling to the early 1790s and it may well be by a Cork plasterer working in the style of neoclassical architect James Wyatt.

However, the marriage settlement was not enough to complete the building work on the house, in part owing to Margaretta leaving Glin to go and live with her half brother back in England, at Forde Abbey and Combe Florey. Debts came piling in and Colonel John found himself unable to finish

ABOVE: *An Irish table settle, which can be either seat or table.*

LEFT: *An Irish vernacular cabinet in the family entrance hall.*

OPPOSITE: *Desmond and Veronica FitzGerald, the present Knight's parents on their wedding day in 1929; old family letters; a photograph of Consuelo, Duchess of Marlborough, great aunt of the present knight's mother; and the 28th Knight's diary are among the ephemera found in the house.*

PRECEDING PAGES:
*The library, with a
portrait of the 4th Earl
of Dunraven hanging
over the mantel.*

ABOVE: *The de Tuyll
family, including the
grandmother of Olda
FitzGerald, the present
Knight's wife.*

RIGHT: *The 4th Earl
of Dunraven, great
grandfather of the
present Knight of Glin.*

OPPOSITE: *Chinoserie is
displayed on the neoclassical
marble chimneypiece in the
library.*

the house; the top floor was left an
open space for nearly two hundred
years, until it was converted
into five more bedrooms and
bathrooms ten years ago. In 1803
Colonel John died, and in order
to pay his debts all the household
furniture, the books from the
library, and a "superb service of
Indian china," (but no pictures or
silver) were sold at a sheriff's sale,
advertised in the local newspaper.

The long minority of John's
son, John Fraunceis, and the fact
that he was an only child, enabled
the estate to survive until 1812,
when he attained his majority.
Educated in England, he is said
to have restored the family
fortunes by successful gambling
and further sales of land. He was

able to build three Gothic lodges, a walled garden, a hermitage, and a battlemented farmyard. He further landscaped the park, submerging the newly built road in the form of a massive ha-ha (a ditch with a retaining wall) by the River Shannon. Nash's pupil, James Pain, built the Board of the First Fruits Church by the entrance to the demesne in 1816 and he probably gingered up the house at this time with the mullioned windows, battlements, and such. John Fraunceis also changed the name from Glin House to Glin Castle in keeping with its new status. This was typical of the romantic notions of the 1820s—he obviously thought that the holder of such an ancient title should be living in a castle like his medieval ancestors.

Little else was done to Glin during the Victorian period as money was scarce. This may have been a blessing in disguise for there were few Victorian "improvements" at Glin that might have altered its character, though the Dublin firm of Sibthorpe redecorated the ceilings.

When Desmond FitzGerald and his wife, Veronica, came to live at Glin in the 1930s, they did much to restore the castle that had fallen into considerable neglect owing to Desmond's father being an invalid. Desmond had poor health and some time after his death Veronica married Canadian magnate Ray Milner; together they put

the place to rights. Since that time, Glin has often been let and received guests and hosted weddings and events. Desmond's son, another Desmond and his wife, Olda, turned the castle into an exclusive place to stay for paying guests and over the years they have completely restored the house and wing. They continue to make it a family home for their children and grandchildren, while regularly hosting and entertaining people from all over the world.

ABOVE: *FitzJohn, the 27th Knight of Glin, with his best man, Captain Charles Wyndham of the royal yacht Osborne taken at his wedding to Lady Rachel Wyndham Quin in 1897.*

OPPOSITE: *A guest bathroom is hung with family photographs.*

PRECEDING PAGES: *The blue bedroom contains a four-poster bed and blue-and-white porcelain*

Lisnavagh

COUNTY CARLOW

They had tried to sell the house in the 1940s, one interested party being Evelyn Waugh, though he eventually decided not to buy the "early Victorian Baronial pile." Fortunately, the house did not sell and in its present size makes an extremely comfortable home.

A magnificent deep-pink rhododendron tree greets visitors to Lisnavagh, the home of the Bunbury family since 1669. The six small children that play in the extensive gardens and grounds surrounding the house are the twelfth generation to have lived there. The house lies on a gently raised plateau with far-reaching views across a well-wooded park to the Blackstairs and Wicklow mountains. The present Tudor Revival house, which replaced its Georgian predecessor, was built in 1847 to designs by the Scottish architect Daniel Robertson for Captain William McClintock Bunbury, a Member of Parliament. Robertson had designed Carrigglas Manor, Co. Longford, a few years earlier in a similar Gothic Tudor Revival style for the Lord Chief Justice of Ireland, Thomas Langlois Lefroy. Lefroy was a cousin of Bunbury's sister-in-law and the inspiration for a famous romantic hero, Mr. Darcy in Jane Austen's *Pride and Prejudice.*

Neither Bunbury nor Robertson would quite recognize the house today; during the postwar years, when large houses were

often seen as an anachronism, the main reception rooms were demolished and rooms in the former service wing became the main reception area. A gabled section with a bay window was moved to cover up the hole in what turned out to be a highly successful remodeling.

Naval relics abound in the house, one of which is a bureau-bookcase in the hall made from the exotic timber of HMS *Samarang.* This was the ship that the young William McClintock Bunbury sailed on while chasing slave ships and protecting British interests in the Southern Hemisphere. In Brazil and Peru, the *Samarang* encountered HMS *Beagle*, upon which Charles Darwin was making his epic five-year voyage

ABOVE: *The garden front of Lisnavagh.*

OPPOSITE: *Children run through the rhododendron grove.*

PRECEDING PAGES: *Old luggage stands beside a Victorian decoupage screen.*

OVERLEAF: *The sunny entry hall contains relics of former generations of Bunburys, including antique parasols and a bookcase made with wood from HMS Samarang.*

The carved oak bookcases in the library frame family portraits, including one of Anne Lefroy, wife of the 1st Lord Rathdonnell (above).

OPPOSITE: *The embossed leather wall covering around the mantelpiece was taken from a four-panel screen.*

around the world. Also on board the *Samarang* was Bunbury's first cousin Francis Leopold McClintock, who later found fame as commander of the steamship *Fox*, sent out in 1857 by Lady Franklin to discover the fate of her husband, Sir John Franklin, the Arctic explorer who had gone missing twelve years earlier.

Captain William McClintock Bunbury's son Thomas inherited Lisnavagh in 1866 on his father's death. Thomas had the added fortune of becoming the 2nd Baron Rathdonnell in 1879 on the death of his father's brother, John, 1st Baron Rathdonnell, inheriting not only the title, but also a vast estate. Portraits of John; his wife, Anne Lefroy; and his brother, William McClintock Bunbury, dressed in his naval uniform, all hang in recesses in the present-day library. That of Anne can be spied in an old black-and-white photograph of the library in its previous incarnation as part of the grand suite of reception rooms in Robertson's original house. Also captured in the photograph is a four-leaf embossed leather screen that now forms the wall covering around the mantelpiece in a highly effective decorative manner. The stripped oak bookcases, which form a warm and inviting backdrop to the room, appear to be made up from a combination of old seventeenth-century paneling and moldings and nineteenth-century cabinetwork. Executed in the antiquarian manner for

the library in Robertson's original house, these were moved into the present room when the house was reduced in size. They could easily be from the Dublin firm of Strahan which supplied much of the original furniture, including the octagonal center table, two writing tables, and set of chairs in the library.

The present Baron Rathdonnell, who succeeded his father, the 4th Baron Rathdonnell, in 1959, jokingly points out of the library window and says: "I was born over there, about 18 feet up in the air." He is referring, of course, to a bedroom that no longer exists, part of the wing pulled down by his parents. They had tried to sell the house in the 1940s, one interested party being Evelyn Waugh, though eventually

he decided not to buy the "early Victorian Baronial pile." Fortunately, the house did not sell and in its present size makes an extremely comfortable home. Lord Rathdonnell now lives with his wife in a new house that they have built within the demesne walls, its design based on a Georgian rectory. Having run Lisnavagh since he was twenty-one, he passed the care of the house to his son, William; his daughter-in-law, Emily; and their two children. They run the house as a venue for weddings and events, for which the principal rooms have undergone a sensitive redecoration. Cleverly mixing the old with the new, two magnificent four-poster beds have delicate passementerie seamlessly combined with modern fabrics. Artifacts

ABOVE: *The Colonel's Room, named after Colonel Kane Bunbury who died at Lisnavagh at ninety-seven.*

OPPOSITE, CLOCKWISE FROM TOP LEFT: *Lively illustrations and humorous verse in a hunting journal from the 1930s and 1940s that belonged to Golly Drew, Lord Rathdonnell's aunt. Passementerie hanging from the four-poster bed in the Colonel's Room. A circular family photograph of Katherine Anne, Lady Rathdonnell, and her eldest son, Billy, who was killed in the Boer War at twenty-one. A pair of Victorian opera glasses.*

relating to various ancestors fill the house: old military coats, hunting boots, ladies' parasols, crested silver, a commemorative foundation trowel, hunting pictures, visitors books, hand-painted photograph albums, and a Victorian decoupage screen. These relics prompt family stories, such as the collection of old swords reminding the Bunburys of a former heir, Billy, who lost his life during the Boer War in 1900. His portrait in his uniform as a 2nd Lieutenant in the Royal Scots Greys hangs in the entrance hall.

Beyond the public gaze, two authors beaver away in the attic: Tom Sykes, William's brother-in-law, and Turtle, his younger brother. A travel writer and historian (Turtle's name originated from a childhood obsession with the four-legged reptile), his books include the acclaimed *Vanishing Ireland* and *Vanishing Ireland: Further Chronicles of a Disappearing World*. It is his children, along with Tom's and William's, that now run around the gardens so lovingly restored to their former glory by the present Lady Rathdonnell.

RIGHT: *A collection of hats adorn a pair of deer antlers.*

BELOW: *Croquet mallets propped against the hall wall.*

OPPOSITE: *The present Lord Rathdonnell's grandmother, Edith Sylvia Drew, filled her photograph album with souvenirs of her travels. The owl is delivering Golly Drew in 1916.*

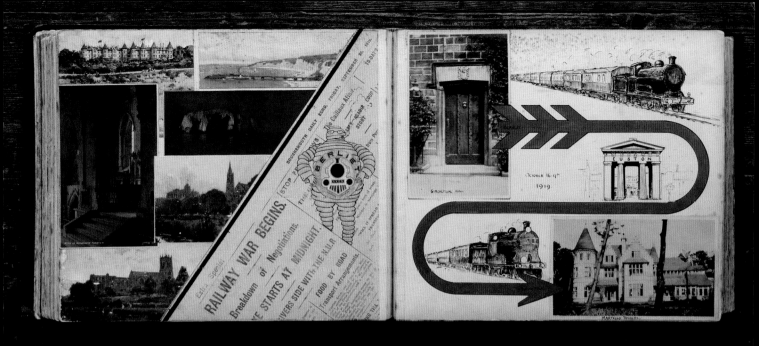

RAILWAY WAR BEGINS.

Breakdown of Negotiations.

STRIKE STARTS AT MIDNIGHT.

DRIVERS SIDE WITH THE N.U.R.

FOOD BY ROAD

EUSTON

OCTOBER 16-4th
1919

SIMONSTONE HALL

MARTELLO TOWERS.

W Peart Robinson

Edith L. Robinson.

Edith Sylvia Drew.
née Peart-Robinson.

Dorothy Peart-Robinson.

Esmond P. Robinson.

Ivo Robinson — His mark. TWHHSFW.

Vivian Peart-Robinson.

Aubyn Peart Robinson.

Angela Peart Robinson.

DALLAM TOWER.
FEBRUARY 18th–20th 1916.

Roderick Williams

Dorothy Peart Robinson

Vivian P. Robinson

FOOD CONTROLLER

Gladys Robinson

Killadoon

COUNTY KILDARE

The stables and outhouses are in a state of "splendid dilapidation," as Charlie philosophically remarks. However, the walled garden is their true joy, cleared and restored by the Clements and once again producing fruit in abundance.

Killadoon is a remarkable survival in every way. Surrounded by a well-wooded park with distant views of the Hill of Lyons, its entrance comes as a surprise, located at the end of a narrow lane backed by the encroaching urban sprawl of Celbridge. It was this congenial location, close to Dublin, that first drew Robert Clements, later 1st Earl of Leitrim, to rent the property from the wealthy Thomas Conolly of nearby Castletown and to build a house here in 1767–71. He was the son of Nathaniel Clements, treasury official, politician, Dublin property developer, amateur architect, failed banker, and leader of fashion, who had amassed a huge fortune from office, and over the years put together an 85,000-acre estate in Counties Leitrim, Donegal, and Cavan, becoming one of the richest men in Ireland. Nathaniel was also ranger of the Phoenix Park and the lodge that he built there forms the core of the official residence of the President of Ireland.

From the outside, Killadoon appears to be a modest Georgian villa of fine proportions with little ornamentation apart from the fenestration and central tripartite doorway. However, inside Killadoon there is a sense of grandeur in the noble proportions and detailing of the rooms. This is typical of Irish country houses of the 1760s: generally plain on the exterior with many windows, just as the Georgian terraces of Dublin display little ornament (apart from their door cases and fanlights). This belies the richness of their interiors with extraordinary rococo and neoclassical plasterwork.

Small classical bronzes, souvenirs of Robert's Grand Tour in 1753–54, adorn the principal rooms along with family portraits and much of the original furniture. Pompeo Batoni's portrait of him, painted in Rome in 1754, hung until very recently in the

ABOVE: *Killadoon viewed from across the park.*

OPPOSITE: *An eighteenth-century bronze of the Callipygian Venus was probably a Grand Tour souvenir.*

PRECEDING PAGES: *The entrance front of Killadoon with its service wing on the left.*

137

ABOVE: *A hall chair, c. 1800, painted with the Clements crest and the 2nd Earl of Leitrim's coronet.*

RIGHT: *The frozen poses of Victorian stuffed birds in the hall.*

OPPOSITE: *Off-cuts of wallpaper from the 1820s show the original vivid colors.*

after Mary's death in 1840. Both sisters and Nathaniel were painted by the leading portrait painter of the day, Sir Thomas Lawrence. Nathaniel and Mary undertook two redecorations of the interior: the first around 1805–10, the second around 1825–35. Writing to his son, George, in 1835, Nathaniel admitted:

> *It is certainly not a fine place, nor can it ever be so, for it has not sufficient extent, nor has nature given it those features that are necessary to constitute a fine place. But . . . it is . . . a very comfortable and enjoyable place, . . . and certainly it is now in a very different state from what it was when I first went to live there.*

The house is laid out in a well-conceived and logical plan. The boldly classical entrance hall, with a stone floor and Doric frieze, is dominated by a dramatic Regency swagged pelmet and draped curtains in scarlet moreen with a bold black border. They were discovered rolled up in the attic by the present owners, Charlie and Sally Clements, who reinstated them as part of the restoration of the house. A pair of Irish elk antlers leans precariously over the stone mantelpiece with its pair of Doric columns. Ranged around the walls is a set of Regency mahogany hall chairs with X-frame seats and

dining room. It shows him (very much the connoisseur) resting his arm on a plinth by a bust of Aristotle. Robert was succeeded by his son, Nathaniel, 2nd Earl of Leitrim, in 1804, and the present appearance of the house owes much to the time of him and his wife, Mary. She was one of the Bermingham sisters who traveled extensively on the Continent and were much admired not only for their beauty, but also for their intelligence. Her sister Anne married the 2nd Earl of Charlemont and helped Nathaniel with the decoration of Killadoon

scrolled backs painted with the Clements family crest and coronet. Like much of the furniture, they appear in early inventories of the house, recently transcribed by Sally and Christopher Moore.

The hall leads directly into the drawing room, which is surely one of the great untouched survivals of Irish country house interiors. The room is still hung with its 1820s green-and-gold wallpaper. Off-cuts of this paper, decorated with a spray pattern on a watered ground and showing their original brilliant color, were found in the house, along with samples of the scrolling acanthus border and rope-twist fillet. Magnificent giltwood mirrors with laurel-wreath crestings fill the window piers and were probably introduced in the 1770s by the 1st Earl, possibly from another house. The gilt pelmets topped by urns most likely date from this time, although the sumptuous red-and-gold swagged curtains date from the 1840s. Lady Charlemont was probably responsible for acquiring the Axminster carpet at this time, its corners woven with a monogram of entwined Ls for Leitrim. The room was recently used in the film *Becoming Jane*, starring Anne Hathaway as Jane Austen.

The drawing room leads into the dining room, which is hung in the traditional manner with family portraits. It boasts a splendid eighteenth-century white and green marble mantelpiece and carved overdoors. The rest of the room, however, is relatively plain and the furniture solid but serviceable.

PRECEDING PAGES: *A pair of ancient Irish elk antlers hangs above the classical mantelpiece.*

ABOVE: *The Axminster carpet in the drawing room has entwined Ls, for Leitrim.*

RIGHT: *Detail of a late-eighteenth-century, painted-satinwood armchair.*

OPPOSITE: *When they were purchased in the 1770s, the enormous pier glasses in the drawing room would have been the height of luxury.*

OVERLEAF: *The spacious, art-filled drawing room with its 1820s wallpaper.*

PAGES 146–47: *The dining room laid for a dinner party with the family silver, glass, and china.*

More surprises are found in the upstairs bedrooms. In the middle room is a splendidly draped four-poster bed, its 1878 floral material dressed in the Regency style of its previous hangings. The sumptuous window curtains are en suite. Down the corridor is another bed with brown and mustard glazed calico hangings dating from before 1830, when they were recorded in an inventory. This bed was last used in 1878, when the body of the "wicked" 3rd Earl of Leitrim was laid out for two days before his burial, after being murdered by the tenants on his Donegal estates. He ran these huge estates of over 50,000 acres with strict discipline, which gained him considerable enmity among his tenantry. Several attempts on his life were made and even his funeral was marred by a mob scene as they tried to drag his coffin from the hearse.

Over the last eighteen years Charlie and Sally Clements have made a valiant effort to restore Killadoon. A hundred years ago one hundred people were employed there, so it is an uphill struggle to keep the house going. The stables and outhouses are in a state of "splendid dilapidation," as Charlie philosophically remarks. However, the walled garden is their true joy, cleared and restored by the Clementses and once again producing fruit in abundance. One can only hope that Killadoon, with its unique interior and furnishings, can survive intact to the next generation of Clementses.

ABOVE: *The drapes of the four-poster bed match the window curtains and date from 1878.*

LEFT: *A book, cut glass, and an old photograph adorn the nightstand.*

OPPOSITE: *Detail of antique lace in a bedroom.*

OVERLEAF: *The bedrooms on the top floor have become repositories for all manner of objects including family portraits, broken chairs, and old luggage.*

Tullynally

COUNTY WESTMEATH

From a distance, the house takes on the appearance of a small, fortified town, or a "Camelot of the Gothic Revival," as one author has described it. Inside it is no less inspiring, with a huge Gothic-vaulted hall filling what was once a courtyard.

Tullynally, which lies in the heart of Ireland, is the turreted and crenellated seat of the Pakenhams, a family of soldiers, sailors, and, in more recent times, writers. Its present appearance is the result of a series of aggrandizements that transformed a restrained classical box into the Gothic castle seen today. The Pakenhams first came here in 1655, when English soldier Captain Henry Pakenham swapped the lands he had been granted in Co. Wexford for Tullynally, which means "Hill of Swans" in Irish. It was later known as Pakenham Hall, in obeisance to its owners, until its present custodian, Thomas Pakenham, changed the name back to its more romantic origins.

From a distance, the house takes on the appearance of a small fortified town, or a "Camelot of the Gothic Revival," as one author has described it. Inside it is no less inspiring, with a huge Gothic vaulted hall filling what was once a courtyard. Among the portraits above the dado paneling hangs one of the young Thomas, 2nd Earl of Longford, painted about 1793 in Rome on his Grand Tour by the German artist Philipp Friedrich von Hetsch. Tom, as he was known, employed the architect Francis Johnston to give his ancestral home a Gothic facelift. Work began in 1801 and continued for five years. The novelist Maria Edgeworth on her visit soon after work was complete, wrote: "Lord Longford has finished and furnished his castle which is now really a mansion fit for a nobleman of his fortune . . . the immense Hall so well warmed that the children play in it from morn till night." Maria had reason to comment on the warmth, as it was her father, Richard Lovell Edgeworth, who had designed the central heating system, the first of its kind in Ireland.

Tom's passion for improvements manifested again two decades later when he employed the architect James Shiel to further Gothicize and enlarge the house, no doubt to house his ever-growing brood of children. Seven of them are portrayed in watercolors now hanging in the drawing room with its vibrant crimson walls: three daughters painted with their mother, Georgiana, and four sons painted with the rather submissive family dog. Tom himself was one of eleven children.

Next door in the library, the posthumous portrait of his brother, General Sir Edward Pakenham hangs over the mantelpiece. Ned, as he was affectionately known, was a distinguished soldier and hero of the Peninsular War. He later lost his life in the War of 1812 during the disastrous (for the British) Battle of New Orleans in 1815.

In the library, centuries of Pakenham literary interests line the oak shelves, cocooning guests in the smell of leather and old paper. Each column of shelves is presided over by a bronze bust of a worthy. Devotees of this room included Evelyn Waugh and Sir John Betjeman, both of whom were guests at Tullynally in the 1930s. The literary tradition can be traced as far back as Elizabeth, created 1st Countess of Longford in 1785. Her literary salon in Cavendish Row, Dublin, was where "one was always sure to meet the cleverest people of this country," as a contemporary visitor wrote. In the adjacent dining room hang portraits of Elizabeth; her husband, Thomas, created 1st Baron Longford; her son, Captain Edward Michael, 2nd Baron Longford; and her

In the servants' quarters,
a key (right) to the bells
(below) lists the names of
the rooms to which they are
connected by an ingenious
system of pulls and wires.

BOTTOM: *Leather fire*
buckets lining the corridor
are painted with an L for
Longford below an earl's
coronet.

PRECEDING PAGES:
The recent apple harvest
spread across the cavernous
old kitchen.

OPPOSITE AND OVERLEAF:
The dining room is hung
with family portraits
against wallpaper designed
by A. W. N. Pugin for the
Houses of Parliament.

grandson, Tom, who succeeded her as 2nd Earl of Longford, his father predeceasing him. These Pakenham family portraits, and others of relations, hang against a striking wallpaper designed by Augustus Welby Northmore. Pugin for the Houses of Parliament, which complements the Gothic revival ceiling. The coffered bay window was part of Shiel's additions to Tullynally.

As if the house was still not quite large enough, after Tom's death the trustees of his son, the 3rd Earl of Longford, employed Sir Richard Morrison, another great exponent of the Gothic style, to alter and enlarge the house yet again, this time adding a family wing and joining the main house to the stable block with service wings. One of the remarkable features of Tullynally is the survival of the servants' quarters. To step from the present-day kitchen into the corridor outside is like taking a step back a hundred years into an era when the house was fully staffed with a housekeeper, a butler, footmen, a cook, and numerous maids. The cavernous kitchen boasts a splendid range and jelly machine, the scullery off it is complete with a wooden plate rack over six feet tall. Monogrammed leather fire buckets hang in the corridor, reminders of the days when every large house had its own fire brigade. A little further on, a stuffed bison head hangs below an extensive array of call bells, silent for the past half century, along with a register of the rooms to which each relates. Across the courtyard, the laundry survives with each of its three rooms devoted to a particular part of the process: washing, drying, and ironing. At the top of the house, the children's nursery, now used as the muniments room, still has hooks in the ceiling for a swing upon which the centenarian Lady Mary Clive (née

OPPOSITE, CLOCKWISE FROM TOP LEFT: *A family of llamas now grazes in the kitchen garden, one of the largest in Ireland. A view through a gateway into the flower garden. A sphinx bought by Lord Longford in 1780 guards the gateway to the kitchen garden. The gingerbread house was built by Thomas and Valerie Pakenham for their grand-children.*

BELOW: *The peach house in the kitchen garden.*

Pakenham) can still remember swinging on as a child.

Thomas Pakenham took over the house from his uncle, Edward, 6th Earl of Longford, forty-eight years ago and as such can claim the longest tenure. He and his wife, Valerie, are well-known authors. Thomas's writing has taken him to the far reaches of the world for books including *The Boer War* and *The Scramble for Africa*. More recently, he has transformed his passion for trees into a series of books commencing with *Meetings with Remarkable Trees*. Each volume is illustrated with his own superb photographs, more often than not scaled with a member of his family standing beneath the great boughs. Thomas has done much to revive the

extensive gardens and pleasure grounds. An intrepid traveler, he has been on several plant hunting expeditions in such places as Yunnan and Tibet, bringing home seeds that have been planted in new gardens. His daughter Eliza has continued the literary tradition with *Tom, Ned and Kitty*, a lively account of her Pakenham ancestors (Kitty married the great Duke of Wellington), set against the backdrop of the Napoleonic wars and Irish insurgencies. Eliza is married to Alex Chisholm, who set up and runs Heritage Gardening, a company specializing in rare and historic bulbs, thereby continuing the family gardening tradition. Their children now run around the grounds of Tullynally, another generation growing up on the Hill of Swans.

Clandeboye

COUNTY DOWN

*M*ore and more roof specialists have been called in to take a look at it. They potter about among the chimneys for many weeks and almost invariably put their foot through its comparatively sound patches before they declare it hopeless.

A relatively modern, white-painted Doric portico on an ostensibly classical facade gives no sense of what happens on the other side of the front door. This is the enchanted world of the great proconsul Frederick Hamilton-Temple-Blackwood, the 1st Marquess of Dufferin and Ava, who was Viceroy of India and Governor General of Canada and held many other important posts.

Up a flight of steps from the front door is the outer hall, flanked by a parade of curling stones and all manner of relics, including Egyptian granite sculptures and tablets, a mummy case, a pair of Indian sculptures, iron cannon, and a Burmese bell. The walls are lined with wire netting hung with a battery of arms and armor interspersed with dusty standards. The floor is covered by a pair of ferocious tiger skins, their mouths open in a roar. Deep crimson curtains mark the passage to the inner hall, where guests walk in trepidation between a pair of stuffed bears holding wooden platters.

The focal point of the space is a great heraldic stained-glass window with the arms of the various families connected with

the Blackwoods, owners of Clandeboye, while further weapons and shields cloak the walls. Over the huge stone fireplace hangs a portrait of the 1st Marquess, as Baron Dufferin, at age twenty-three. One could be mistaken for thinking the portrait shows Sir Galahad in the trappings of an Irish baron. The Marquess loved the novels of the great Romantic Scottish author Sir Walter Scott, and confessed: "I love Sir Walter Scott with all my heart; and my mother excepted, I think he has done more to form

ABOVE: *The south front of Clandeboye glimpsed from across the park.*

OPPOSITE: *The inner hall hung with arms and armor collected by the 1st Marquess of Dufferin and Ava.*

PRECEDING PAGES: *The view from the roof of Helen's Tower across the fields of County Down.*

my character than any other influence; for he is the soul of purity, chivalry, respect for women and healthy religious feeling." Another influence on the impressionable young man must have been the Eglinton Tournament of 1839, a reenactment of a medieval joust, at which his aunt, Lady Seymour, was Queen of Beauty.

The house's dramatic entrance was created out of the former scullery and kitchen, enabling the original hall and adjoining study to be combined into a spacious and inviting library. However, these changes are minor compared to the megalomaniacal plans to rebuild the house drawn up by a series of architects: William Burn proposed enlarging and refacing the house in red brick in the Elizabethan style; Benjamin Ferrey produced designs in the Scottish baronial manner; and William Henry Lynn favored the Scotch Jacobean with definite French Renaissance overtones, as well as a completely new house overlooking Belfast Lough. Needless to say, owing to monetary restrictions, none of these plans were executed. One of Lord Dufferin's plans that did come to fruition was Helen's Tower, a folly designed by Burn in the Scottish baronial style in 1848 as an offering to his mother when he came of age. Alfred, Lord Tennyson wrote a dedicatory poem, which began:

Helen's Tower here I stand
Dominant over sea and land.
Son's love built me, and I hold
Mother's love in lettered gold.

Behind the dramatic entry halls in the house lies a rabbit warren of service rooms, reminders of the days when the house had twenty indoor staff and many more outside. This must have been the part of the house that reminded Lord Dufferin's descendant, Caroline Blackwood, of her childhood home when she wrote in her novel *Great Granny Webster* of the eternal problems and mystical importance of Irish roofs due to the incessant rain: "More and more roof specialists have been called in to take a look at it. They potter about among the chimneys for many weeks and almost invariably put their foot through its comparatively sound patches before they declare it hopeless."

The house was originally called Ballyleidy and had been the home of the Blackwoods since the seventeenth century, first as tenants of the Hamiltons and later as owners (Sir John Blackwood, 2nd Baronet married the Hamilton heiress). Between 1800 and about 1820, the previous plain box was replaced by a design by Robert Woodgate, a pupil of Sir John Soane, who had been working at Baronscourt, the Duke of Abercorn's seat, in the last decade of the eighteenth century. Woodgate designed the house to be entered through the Doric portico on the south front, but the library later absorbed the hall there. He also planned a series of large reception rooms opening off a central gallery with an imperial staircase rising up above a copy of Thomas Gainsborough's portrait of Mrs. Richard Brinsley Sheridan. Opposite the staircase is the drawing room, with its shallow

bow-front window looking down to the panorama of woods, lakes, and bridges. The park was laid out by James Fraser, a pupil of J. C. Loudon, who enlarged the existing park, added two lakes, and even moved a public road: "a very difficult business" as Lord Dufferin afterward recalled.

The woods have been brilliantly planted with an amazing series of shrubs and rare species inaugurated by the late Sheridan, 5th and last Marquess of Dufferin and Ava, and continued enthusiastically by his widow, Lindy, who has invigorated the house with new life and energy, following in the footsteps of her mother-in-law, Maureen Guinness. Maureen, whose husband, the 4th Marquess, was killed while on active service in Burma, rescued the house after the Second World War.

Lord and Lady Dufferin have been patrons of many artists, including Francis Bacon and Lucian Freud. Lady Dufferin was a pupil of Oskar Kokoschka and the Bloomsbury artist Duncan Grant. She has painted with Derek Hill, Martin Mooney, and Alec Cobbe. In the former stables, Lady Dufferin recently established the Ava Gallery, which encourages young

RIGHT: *The drawing room on the east side looks out over the park.*

BELOW: *A Victorian marble bust of the 1st Marquess of Dufferin and Ava stands on a column beside the window.*

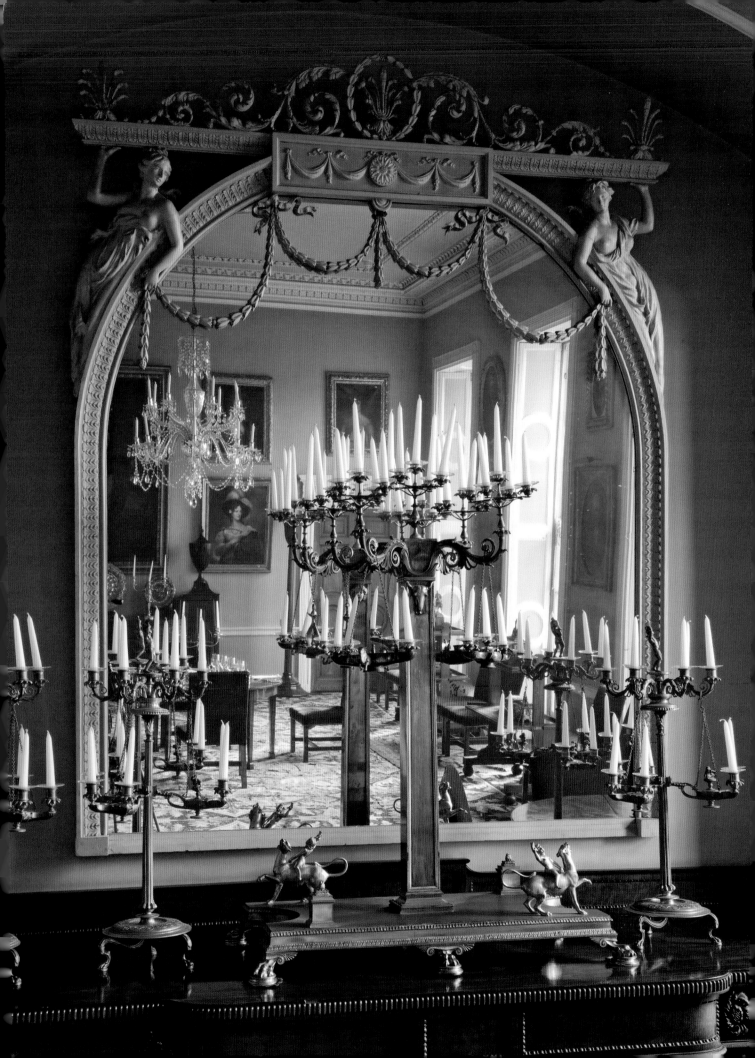

contemporary artists from Northern Ireland. David Hockney was a frequent visitor and Clandeboye has been the subject of some of his work. Lady Dufferin, who paints under her maiden name, Lindy Guinness, has had a number of successful exhibitions at the Browse & Darby Gallery in London. She especially loves painting her cows. From the dairy herd at Clandeboye she has recently started a yogurt business. She is a charming hostess at Clandeboye. The guest bedrooms derive their names from the places where the 1st Marquess was posted, including Burma, Rome, Canada, India, France, and Russia. A blackboard listing the bedrooms, chalked up with the names of the guests and their arrival and departure times, hangs in a back passage.

Today Clandeboye is a lively place with the Conservation Volunteers working (set up by Lady Dufferin and her late husband to promote tree planting all over Northern Ireland), weddings taking place, and the collection and library curated by the indefatigable Lola Armstrong. Lady Dufferin ends the memorable essay "Clandeboye and My Life," in the Ulster and Architectural Heritage Society's history of the house, with these words: "It is a house of dreams and enchantment that fill my thoughts and, as I grow older, the pleasure of being part of it grows greater."

OPPOSITE: *The sideboard alcove in the dining room.*

BELOW: *The dining room at Clandeboye.*

OVERLEAF LEFT: *A detail of a giltwood chair in the Paris bedroom.*

OVERLEAF RIGHT: *Puppets wait patiently in a store room.*

PAGES 188–89: *The guest bedroom called Paris is decorated with a lively mix of bright wallpaper, textiles and furnishings.*

BIBLIOGRAPHY

GENERAL

Bence-Jones, Mark. *A Guide to Irish Country Houses*. Rev. ed. London: Constable, 1988.

Bunbury, Turtle. *The Landed Gentry & Aristocracy of County Wicklow*. Vol. I. Dublin: Irish Family Names, 2005.

Burke, Sir Bernard. *A Genealogical and Heraldic History of the Landed Gentry of Ireland*. London: Harrison, 1912.

Cornforth, John. "Tourism and Irish Houses," *Country Life*, 6 May 1976, pp. 1154–56.

Dooley, Terence. *The Decline of the Big House in Ireland*. Dublin: Wolfhound Press, 2001.

Gray, Tony. *A Peculiar Man, A Life of George Moore*. London: Sinclair Stevenson, 1996.

Heron, Marianne, and Walter Pfeiffer. *In the Houses of Ireland*. London: Thames & Hudson, 1988.

McBride, Simon, and Karen Howes. *Private Ireland*. London: Scriptum Editions, 1999.

Montgomery-Massingberd, Hugh, and Christopher Simon Sykes. *Great Houses of Ireland*. London: Laurence King, 1999.

Mosley, Charles, ed. *Burke's Peerage, Baronetage & Knightage*. 107th ed., 3 vols. Switzerland: Morris Genealogical Books, 2003.

O'Brien, Jacqueline, and Desmond Guinness. *Great Irish Houses and Castles*. London: Weidenfeld & Nicolson, 1992.

Olbricht, Klaus-Hartmut, and Helga M. Wegener. *Irish Houses*. Dublin: Gill and Macmillan, 1984 (German edition 1982).

BIRR CASTLE

Girouard, Mark. "Birr Castle, Co. Offaly–I," *Country Life*, 25 Feb 1965, pp. 410–14.

———. "Birr Castle, Co. Offaly–II," *Country Life*, 4 Mar 1965, pp. 468–471.

———. "Birr Castle, Co. Offaly–II," *Country Life*, 11 Mar 1965, pp. 526–27.

Laffan, William, ed. *Miscelanea Structura Curiosa by Samuel Chearnley*. Tralee: Churchill House Press, 2005.

Malcomson, A. P. W., ed. *Calendar of The Rosse Papers*. Dublin: Irish Manuscripts Commission, 2008.

Pym, Horace N., ed. *Memories of Old Friends, Being Extracts from the Journals and Letters of Caroline Fox of Penjerrick, Cornwall from 1835–1871*. London: Smith, Elder & Co., 1882.

Waterson, Merlin, ed. *The Country House Remembered, Recollections of Life between the Wars*. London: Routlege & Kegan Paul, 1985.

BURTOWN HOUSE

Bunbury, Turtle and Art Kavanagh. *The Landed Gentry & Aristocracy of County Kildare*. Dublin: Irish Family Names, 2004, pp. 73–84.

CLANDEBOYE

Bence-Jones, Mark. "The Building Dreams of a Viceroy–I," *Country Life*, 1 October 1970, pp. 816–19.

Brett, C. E. B. *Buildings of North County Down*. Belfast: Ulster Architectural Heritage Society, 2002, pp. 94–95.

Dean, Ptolemy, "Forgotten genius, Clandeboye House, Co. Down–I," *Country Life*, 2 Dec 2009, pp. 48–51.

———. "An imperial adventure, Clandeboye House, Co. Down—II," *Country Life*, 9 Dec 2009, pp. 46-51.

Rankin, Peter. *Clandeboye*. Belfast: Ulster Architectural Heritage Society, 1985.

GLIN CASTLE

Browne, Father Francis, S. J. "Glin Castle," *Irish Tatler and Sketch*, Dec 1949, pp. 15-22.

Cornforth, John. "Glin Castle, Co. Limerick," *Country Life*, 11 June 1998, pp. 166-73.

Girouard, Mark. "Glin Castle, Co, Limerick—I," *Country Life*, 27 Feb 1964, pp. 446-58.

———. "Glin Castle, Co, Limerick—II," *Country Life*, 27 Feb 1964, pp. 502-05.

The Knight of Glin. "Glin," *Bulletin of the Irish Georgian Society*, Vol. II, no. 3, 1959, pp. 30-40.

———. "Glin Castle," *Archaeological Journal*, Vol. 153, 1996, p. 326.

———. "The Treasures of Glin Castle," *The World of Hibernia*, Spring 1996, pp. 154-72.

KILLADOON

Cornforth, John. "Killadoon, Co. Kildare," *Country Life*, 15 January 2004, pp. 46-51 and 22 January 2004, pp. 54-57.

Malcomson, A. P. W. *Nathaniel Clements, Government and the Governing Elite in Ireland, 1725-75*. Dublin: Four Courts Press, 2005.

———. *Virtues of a Wicked Earl: The Life and Legend of William Sydney Clements, 3rd Earl of Leitrim (1806-78)*. Dublin: Four Courts Press, 2009.

KILLRUDDERY

Bunbury, Turtle. *The Landed Gentry & Aristocracy of County Wicklow*. Vol. 1. Dublin: Irish Family Names, 2005, pp. 24-51.

Comyn, Brendan. "Killruddery House," unpublished thesis, Institute of Professional Auctioneers and Valuers, 1989.

The Knight of Glin and John Cornforth. "Killruddery, Co. Wicklow," *Country Life*, 14 July 1977, pp. 78-81 and 21 July 1977, pp. 146-149.

Malins, Edward, and the Knight of Glin. *Lost Demesnes*. London: Barrie & Jenkins, 1976.

TARBERT HOUSE

Gaughan, J. Anthony. *Listowel and its Vicinity, Cork*. Cork: Mercier Press, 1973, pp. 528-32 and 534-36.

Hickson, Mary Agnes. *Selections from Old Kerry Records*. London, 1872, pp. 325-27.

Holly, Denis, and Josephine Holly. *Tarbert on the Shannon*. Ballyshannon: Donegal Democrat, 1961, p. 28.

Hussey de Burgh, U. H. *The Landowners of Ireland*. Dublin, 1878, p. 269.

The Knight of Glin. "Tarbert House, Co. Kerry," *Irish Arts Review*, Autumn 2006, pp. 106-109.

Laffan, William, ed. *Painting Ireland: Topographical Views from Glin Castle*. Tralee: Churchill House Press, 2006, pp. 94-97.

Pielou, Pierce Leslie. *The Leslies of Tarbert and Their Forebears*. Dublin: Brindleys, 1935.

TULLYNALLY

Pakenham, Eliza. *Tom, Ned and Kitty*. London: Phoenix, 2008.

The doors of the Georgian bookcase in the study at Killadoon are screened with chicken wire to protect the books.

PAGE 192:

A curtain and an Irish table in the dining room at Tullynally.

Dedicated to our wives
Joanna Fennell, Olda FitzGerald, and Saskia Peill

———

ACKNOWLEDGMENTS

William and Emily Bunbury, Turtle Bunbury,
Charlie and Sally Clements, Lindy Dufferin, Lesley Fennell,
William Laffan, Ursula Leslie, Jack and Xenia Meath,
Thomas and Valerie Pakenham, Ben and Jessica Rathdonnell,
Moira Durdin-Robertson, Brendan and Alison Rosse,
Miranda Willes

On the cover: Burtown House, County Kildare

First published in the United Kingdom in 2010 by Thames & Hudson Ltd,
181A High Holborn, London WC1V 7QX

This paperback edition first published in 2012

British Library Cataloguing-in-Publication Data
A catalogue record for this book is available from the British Library

ISBN: 978-0-500-29022-4

Printed and bound in China

To find out about all our publications, please visit www.thamesandhudson.com.
There you can subscribe to our e-newsletter, browse or download our current
catalogue, and buy any titles that are in print.